W9-BXX-927

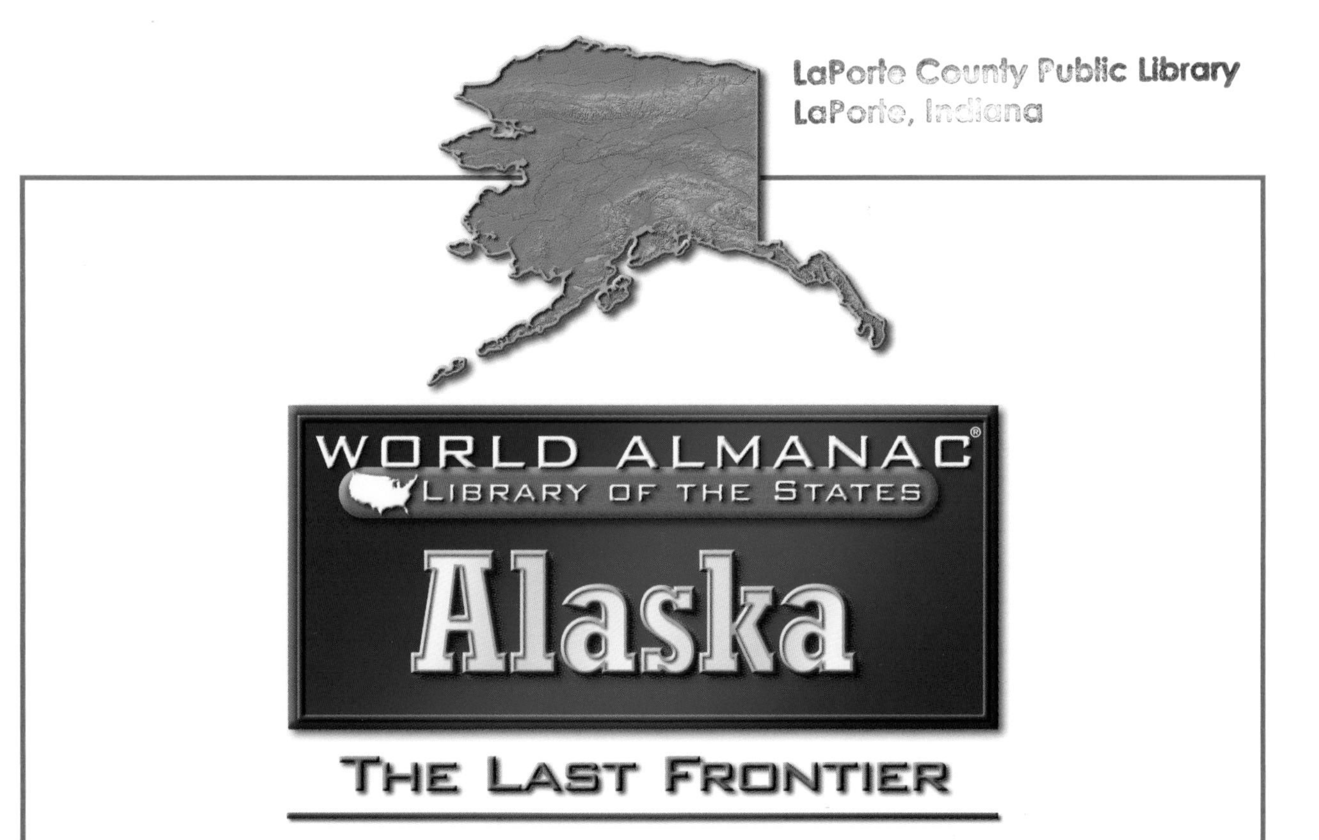

Alaska

THE LAST FRONTIER

by Isaac Seder

WORLD ALMANAC® LIBRARY

Please visit our web site at: www.worldalmanaclibrary.com
For a free color catalog describing World Almanac® Library's list of high-quality books and multimedia programs, call 1-800-848-2928 (USA) or 1-800-387-3178 (Canada).
World Almanac® Library's fax: (414) 332-3567.

Library of Congress Cataloging-in-Publication Data

Seder, Isaac.
Alaska, the last frontier / by Isaac Seder.
p. cm. — (World Almanac Library of the states)
Includes bibliographical references and index.
Summary: Text and illustrations present the history, geography, people, politics and government, economy, customs, and attractions of Alaska.
ISBN 0-8368-5147-1 (lib. bdg.)
ISBN 0-8368-5318-0 (softcover)
1. Alaska—Juvenile literature. [1. Alaska.] I. Title. II. Series.
F904.3.S43 2003
979.8—dc21 2002191073

First published in 2003 by
World Almanac® Library
330 West Olive Street, Suite 100
Milwaukee, WI 53212 USA

A Creative Media Applications Production
Design: Alan Barnett, Inc.
Copy editor: Laurie Lieb
Fact checker: Joan Verniero
Photo researcher: Linette Mathewson
World Almanac® Library project editor: Tim Paulson
World Almanac® Library editors: Mary Dykstra, Gustav Gedatus, Jacqueline Laks Gorman, Lyman Lyons
World Almanac® Library art direction: Tammy Gruenewald
World Almanac® Library graphic designers: Scott M. Krall, Melissa Valuch

Photo credits: pp. 4-5 © Paul Souders/Danita Delimont, Agent; p. 6 (top right) © ArtToday; p. 6 (bottom left) © George D. Lepp/CORBIS; p. 6 (bottom right) © Les Campbell; p. 7 (top) © Royalty-Free/CORBIS; p. 7 (bottom) © Royalty-Free/CORBIS; p. 9 © Hulton Archive/Getty Images; p. 10 © Hulton Archive/Getty Images; p. 11 © CORBIS; p. 12 © Hulton Archive/Getty Images; p. 13 © North Wind Picture Archives; p. 14 © AP/Wide World Photos; p. 15 © Photri, Inc.; p. 17 © Paul Souders/Danita Delimont, Agent; p. 18 © Stuart Westmoreland/Danita Delimont, Agent; p. 19 © Photri, Inc.; p. 20 (left) © Danny Lehman/CORBIS; p. 20 (center) © Buddy Mays; p. 20 (right) © AP/Wide World Photos; p. 21 (left) © Danita Delimont; p. 21 (center) © Royalty-Free/CORBIS; p. 21 (right) © Stuart Westmoreland/Danita Delimont, Agent; p. 23 © Paul Souders/Danita Delimont, Agent; p. 26 © Kevin Fleming/CORBIS; p. 27 © Jeff Greenburg/Danita Delimont, Agent; p. 29 © Photri, Inc.; p. 31 (top) © AP/Wide World Photos; p. 31 (bottom) © Photri, Inc.; p. 32 © Jeff Greenburg/Danita Delimont, Agent; p. 33 © Hugh S. Rose/Danita Delimont, Agent; p. 34 © Paul Souders/Danita Delimont, Agent; p. 35 © Photri, Inc.; p. 36 © Photri, Inc.; p. 37 (top) © AP/Wide World Photos; p. 37 (bottom) © AP/Wide World Photos; p. 38 © Hulton Archive/Getty Images; p. 39 (left) © North Wind Picture Archives; p. 39 (right) © Hulton Archive/Getty Images; p. 40 © Hulton Archive/Getty Images; p. 41 (top) © AP/Wide World Photos; p. 41 (bottom) © AP/Wide World Photos; pp. 42-43 © North Wind Picture Archives; p. 44 (top) © AP/Wide World Photos; p. 44 (bottom) © Jeff Greenburg/Danita Delimont, Agent; p. 45 (top) © Photri, Inc.; p. 45 (bottom) © Buddy Mays

Printed in the United States of America

1 2 3 4 5 6 7 8 9 07 06 05 04 03

Alaska

A Superlative State

Alaska is a state of superlatives. It is the largest state, more than twice the size of Texas, but it has one of the smallest populations. Alaska not only contains Point Barrow, the northernmost point in North America, but also — thanks to the Aleutian Island chain — both the westernmost (Amatignak Island), and the easternmost (Pochnoi Point on Semisopochnoi Island) points in North America. Seventeen of North America's tallest mountains are also found in Alaska.

There are 6,640 miles (10,684 kilometers) of coastline in Alaska, more than in the rest of all the other states combined. Alaskan waters teem with fish, making its fishing industry the most productive in the nation. Alaska's interior water fills three million lakes and flows in more than three thousand rivers. Meanwhile, miles of frozen water shift slowly in one of Alaska's most famous landscape features — its more than one hundred thousand glaciers. Two of these, the Bering and the Malaspina glaciers, each cover more land area than the state of Delaware.

Alaska is not just big, it's geologically active, too. About one-quarter of all earthquake energy released worldwide has its epicenter in Alaska, and nearly 80 percent of the active volcanoes in the United States are located there. Wildlife in Alaska provides another set of astonishing superlatives, from the world's largest group of bald eagles to its variety of large mammals, including whales, grizzly bears, seals, and wolves.

Alaska's unique and fascinating history reflects many different cultures. Alaska has been shaped by Native Alaskans, the Russians who established the first European settlements in the eighteenth century, and those who made the long trek north to find gold. Settlers who fell in love with the deeper richness of Alaska stayed. Today's Alaskans treasure their state's resources and seek to maintain its truly superlative environment.

▶ Map of Alaska showing the interstate highway system, as well as major cities and waterways.

▼ The Kenai Glacier sparkles on the south Alaskan coast.

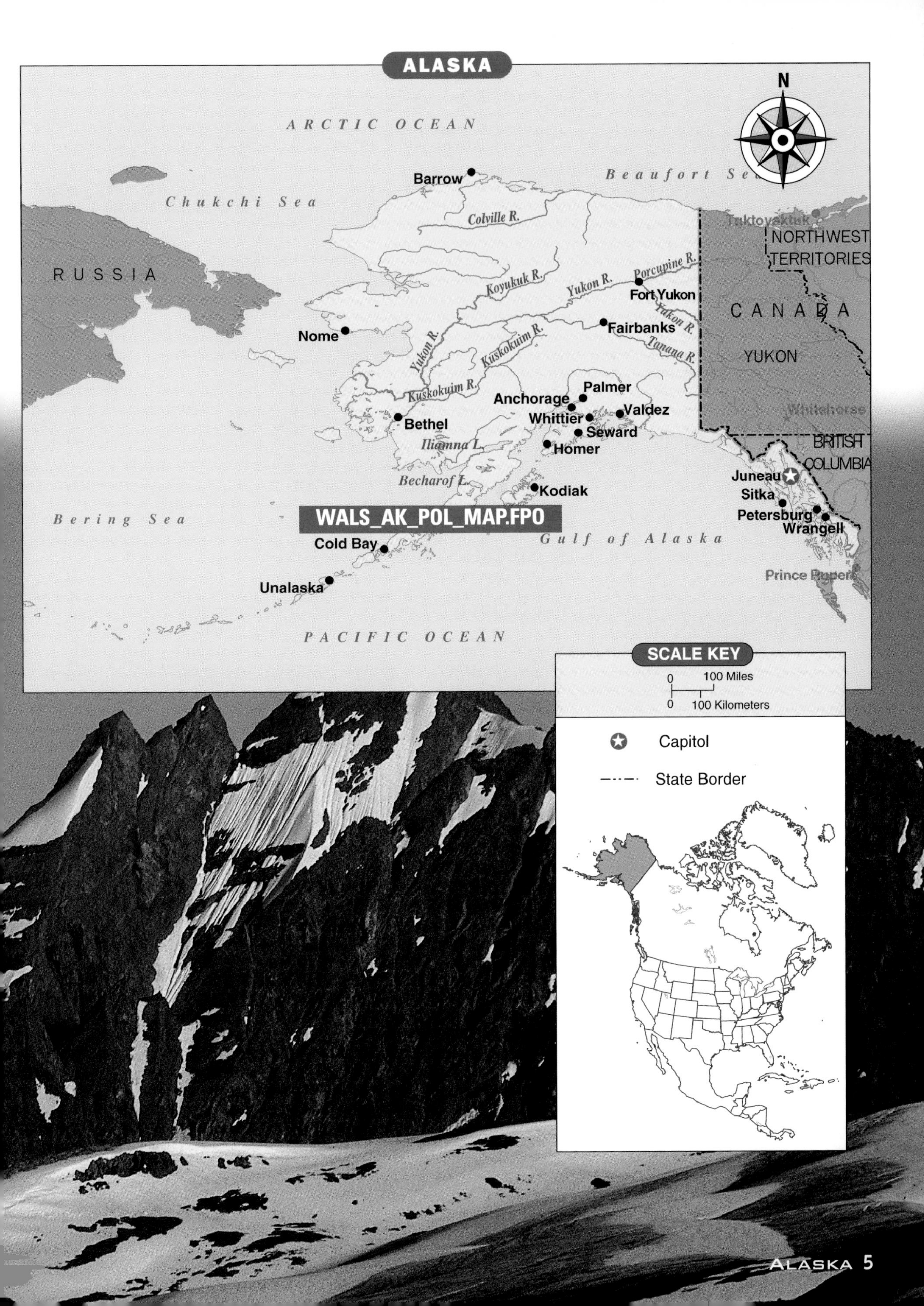
ALASKA
ARCTIC OCEAN
Beaufort Sea
Chukchi Sea
RUSSIA
Barrow
Colville R.
Tuktoyaktuk
NORTHWEST TERRITORIES
Porcupine R.
Koyukuk R.
Yukon R.
Fort Yukon
CANADA
Fairbanks
Yukon R.
Tanana R.
Nome
Yukon R.
Kuskokwim R.
YUKON
Kuskokwim R.
Palmer
Anchorage
Valdez
Whittier
Whitehorse
Bethel
Seward
Iliamna L.
Homer
BRITISH COLUMBIA
Becharof L.
Juneau
Kodiak
Sitka
Bering Sea
WALS_AK_POL_MAP.FPO
Petersburg
Wrangell
Cold Bay
Gulf of Alaska
Prince Rupert
Unalaska
PACIFIC OCEAN
N
SCALE KEY
0 100 Miles
0 100 Kilometers
Capitol
State Border

ALASKA (AK), The Last Frontier

Entered Union

January 3, 1959 (49th state)

Capital	Population
Juneau	30,711

Total Population (2000)

626,932 (48th most populous state) – *Between 1990 and 2000, the state's population increased 14 percent.*

Largest Cities	Population
Anchorage	260,283
Juneau	30,711
Fairbanks	30,224
Sitka	8,835
Ketchikan	7,922

Land Area

571,951 square miles (1,481,353 square km) (the largest state)

State Motto

"North to the Future"

State Song

"Alaska's Flag" *by Marie Drake and Elinor Dusenbury, adopted in 1955.*

State Land Mammal

Moose

State Sea Mammal

Bowhead whale – *In 1983, the Alaskan legislature adopted this sea mammal in recognition of its "grace, strength, and beauty."*

State Bird

Willow ptarmigan – *Found throughout the state, the ptarmigan is known for its changing plumage. The ptarmigan's feathers change from brown to white in winter.*

State Fish

King salmon

State Insect

Four-spot skimmer dragonfly – *This fast-flying insect was voted Alaska's insect by public school students in 1995. The dragonfly was just a little more popular than the second-place bug: the mosquito.*

State Flower

Forget-me-not

State Tree

Sitka spruce

State Mineral

Gold

State Fossil

Wooly mammoth

State Sport

Dog mushing – *Dog mushing is a traditional way to traverse Alaska's vast distances. Races like the Iditarod often follow paths used by mushers of the past.*

PLACES TO VISIT

Denali National Park and Preserve,
near Denali Park
Alaska's most visited national park offers visitors a unique opportunity to view soaring mountains and an astonishing variety of wildlife, from eagles and Dall sheep to bears, moose, and caribou.

Ketchikan Totems, *Ketchikan*
Visitors to the Totem Heritage Center view the largest exhibit of authentic totems in the United States.

Glacier Bay National Park and Preserve,
west of Juneau
Tourists and Alaskans alike visit this park to see the stunning snow-capped peaks surrounding glaciers and icy waters, plus many marine animals, including whales, seals, and sea otters.

For other places and events, see p. 44.

BIGGEST, BEST, AND MOST

- The Arctic National Wildlife Refuge covers 19.6 million acres (8 million hectares) — about as much land as Maine.
- At 20,320 feet (6,194 meters), Mount McKinley is the highest mountain in North America.
- Experts estimate that 30 percent of the United States oil reserve lies under Alaskan land.

STATE FIRSTS

- **1974** Thelma Buckholdt is the first Filipino American woman to be elected to a state legislature.
- **1976** Alaska became the first state to eradicate measles and rubella. Because of its thorough vaccination policies, no cases occurred between 1973 and 1976.
- **1985** Alaska became the first state to operate a trade office in Seoul, Korea.
- **1990** Alaska became the first state to give the Green Party a place on the ballot. This political party focuses on conservation and the environment.

Land of the Midnight Sun

Much of Alaska lies very close to the North Pole. During the summer, the Sun in Barrow sets for only two hours. It never gets dark — there are two hours of twilight before the Sun comes up again. During this time, people in the "Land of the Midnight Sun" have to get used to sleeping when it's light outside. Unique festivals celebrate this unusual brightness, with baseball games starting at midnight and running late into the night. Of course, during winter, the Sun barely rises in Barrow, leaving the region in near darkness twenty-four hours a day.

Great Glaciers

A glacier is a huge mass of slowly moving ice. The surface of a glacier is hard and icy, but the lower surface is actually melting and refreezing. Heat from the earth and friction cause the underside to melt, allowing the glacier to move. Alaska has thousands of glaciers, providing opportunities for both scientists and nature lovers. Many glaciers are a striking ice-blue color; others provide easily accessible, spectacular hiking trails.

A Far Frontier

> Of all the moonlights in the world, commend me to those which light up the archipelago of the North Pacific Ocean. The entire region of Oregon, Washington Territory, British Columbia, and Alaska seems thus to become a ship yard for the supply of all nations.
>
> *– William Seward in a speech celebrating the purchase of Alaska, August 29, 1869*

During the Ice Age, Alaska looked very different from how it looks today. Glaciers covered much more of the land than at present, and the outline of the land was very different also. Some regions that are now covered by water were once dry land. Many anthropologists believe that a strip of land connected Russia with Alaska, thus becoming an important migration route.

Prehistoric animals would have been the first to cross such a land bridge. Mammals such as the woolly mammoth and the fierce saber-toothed tiger probably migrated into what is now Alaska in search of food. It is believed that perhaps thirty thousand years ago the first people would have made the same trip. According to this theory, melting glacier water slowly covered the land bridge, and about fourteen thousand years ago, the bridge was completely underwater.

Native Americans of Alaska
Aleut
Athabascan
Haida
Inupiaq Eskimo
Tlingit
Yupik Eskimo

The First Alaskans

The first Alaskans to live along the coast were the Tlingit and the Haida. The mild climate and rich resources helped these coastal tribes survive. The Tlingit lived in Alaska's panhandle, a narrow region that stretches along the state's southeastern coast. These experienced artists used their strong navigation skills to trade with other Native people. After loading their boats with valuable blankets made from dog and goat hair, they would journey 1,000 miles (1,609 km) south to trade with Native people of the Pacific Northwest.

The Haida lived in the southern end of Alaska's panhandle. They came to Alaska from Canada in the early 1700s. Taking advantage of the region's lush forests, the Haida built remarkable canoes. Dug out from a single cedar trunk, these boats were both functional and beautiful. Coastal Natives also built strong clan houses with peaked roofs. Several families lived in each wooden home.

The Aleut also lived near the ocean, but in the foggy southwestern islands now known as the Aleutians. They sailed in amazingly lightweight but stable kayaks called baidarkas. Light enough for a child to carry, these whalebone or driftwood frames covered in sealskin helped Aleuts travel and hunt.

Other Alaskan Native people lived in the huge, harsh interior. The Athabascan often lived in small groups that moved from place to place. They fished for salmon and hunted caribou and bears. They were also among the earliest people to use snowshoes for tromping through the many different types of snowy conditions.

Eskimos lived in northern and western Alaska. The Inupiaq Eskimos settled in the Arctic region. The Yupik Eskimos settled in the west. Both regions experience very harsh, cold winters. During the summer, Eskimos hunted for food that could be stored for the long, dark winter.

DID YOU KNOW?

Both the Tlingit and the Haida marked important events by a ceremony called a potlatch. The person giving the potlatch would prove his wealth by giving away all of his possessions and food. Guests were challenged to give an even more impressive potlatch.

▼ **Native Athabascan living near the Russian settlement at Kotlik in 1895. Traditional Athabascan canoes were made from birch bark, moose hide, and cottonwood.**

Early Alaskans lived for thousands of years in balance with their environment. By the middle of the eighteenth century, that careful balance was about to collapse.

Russians Open the Fur Trade

Peter the Great ruled Russia from 1689 to 1725. Curious to find out what lay beyond the eastern edges of Siberia, Peter appointed Vitus Bering to explore the possible route to America. The fog was so thick during Bering's first voyage in 1728 that he did not realize he had nearly reached the shores of Alaska. He returned home without ever seeing America. On his second voyage in 1741, Bering's ships landed on an island off the Kamchatka Peninsula. Bering became ill and died, but survivors reported their exciting discovery to Russia.

Russian merchants were tempted by Alaska's rich supply of animal furs. They came to Alaska and established a fierce, cruel rule over the Aleut. Russian traders forced the Alaskan Natives to hunt for them. Many Aleut also suffered from diseases brought by the newcomers. The Russian occupation nearly wiped out the Aleut, whose population decreased 80 percent during the first one hundred years of contact with Russia.

Did You Know?

Russian traders often used ruthless strategies to control Alaskan Natives. When Grigor Shelikof arrived at Kodiak Island in 1784, the people living there tried to resist the Russians. Shelikof's response was harsh. After killing many Native men, Shelikof took the surviving women and children hostage. Even after he let the wives return to their husbands, Shelikof kept one child from each family as hostage.

▼ **This group of Inuits or Eskimos was photographed near Point Barrow on the Arctic coast in 1914.**

In 1802, Tlingits who lived near Sitka resisted a Russian trading company that tried to claim land. They attacked the Russian settlement, killing both the Russians and their Aleut slaves. Two years later, the Russians returned and regained the land after a fierce battle. The Tlingits were forced to abandon their land.

Once Russia started to trade Alaskan furs, other countries took an interest in this remote region, which was then called Russian America. Spain, France, and Britain all sent explorers or traders. The new traders forced Native hunters to catch more and more otters, whales, and seals. The populations of these animals plunged as fur traders greedily overhunted.

The Hudson's Bay Company, based in England, was one of the first and most aggressive companies to send traders to Alaska. In 1840, this company negotiated with the Russians in Alaska. It leased a portion of southeastern Alaska and established two trading posts there.

The United States Makes a Deal

Life in Alaska grew increasingly difficult for the Russians. It was getting harder to hunt for furs because so many animals had been killed. Russians had difficulty forming permanent settlements. Despite years of effort, only about nine hundred Russians lived in Alaska by 1867.

At the same time, some people in the United States were becoming more interested in Alaska. They hoped to take advantage of its good fishing and plentiful minerals. In 1859, U.S. Senator William McKendree Gwin of California made an unofficial offer to buy the territory for $5 million. The Russians had not yet accepted the offer when the Civil War began in 1861.

After the Civil War ended, the United States began negotiations again. In 1867, Secretary of State William H. Seward concluded the deal he had negotiated. Authorized by the U.S. Congress, Seward bought the territory for $7.2 million, or about two cents an acre.

Jefferson Randolph "Soapy" Smith

During the Gold Rush years, Alaska was a hard territory to govern. U.S. marshals were often alone as they fought to protect citizens and enforce laws. Some criminals came to Alaska to take advantage of this situation. One of the most notorious, Soapy Smith, arrived in Skagway in 1897. For nine months, Smith and his gang took control of Skagway, having made a deal with the town marshal. Smith swindled money out of the thousands of miners who passed through the town, but he was careful never to swindle the residents of the town. In fact, he became a popular figure, giving away money to the locals in order to earn their support. However, Skagway's reputation grew worse and worse. Soon miners began to avoid the town because they feared meeting Smith. Finally, some residents took the law into their own hands. Soapy Smith's gang was driven out of town, but Smith died in a shootout. He is buried in an unmarked grave in Skagway.

Gold Brings Growth

In the first years after the United States bought Alaska, a few bold pioneers began new businesses. Fishing was the first business to boom in Alaska. Halibut, herring, and salmon were still plentiful. The first salmon canneries opened in 1878.

Fish didn't attract a lot of people, but gold did. In 1896, the discovery of gold in the Canadian Yukon caught everyone's attention. The easiest way to reach the site was by taking a boat to the Alaskan coastal town of Skagway. In just weeks, over one hundred thousand people rushed to Skagway, dreaming of endless wealth.

Alaska's permanent population began to boom. In addition to mining and fishing, newcomers established restaurants, hotels, stores, and other services for the people of a growing Alaska.

Steps to Statehood

Politicians realized that Alaska needed firmer rule. They created a civil code of law in 1900. Juneau was named the state capital in the same year. Alaskans sent their first delegate to the U.S. House of Representatives in 1906. He was not given the right to vote, however. In 1912, Congress passed the Second Organic Act for Alaska, making the region an official territory. Many Alaskans viewed this as a positive step toward statehood. The growth to statehood was

Seward's Folly

Some people thought that buying Alaska was a ridiculous idea. They thought that Russians had taken everything valuable in Alaska, leaving nothing but ice and hardship. Many editorials suggested that the United States had wasted millions of dollars for this useless land. Critics came up with many nicknames to show their disapproval. Some called Alaska "Seward's Folly" or "Seward's Icebox." Others named it "Walrussia."

▼ **Although most of the Alaskan pioneers seeking gold in the 1890s were men, some women and children also made the difficult journey.**

strongly supported by growing local businesses, such as canneries.

Alaska's government showed a progressive nature in its early years. In 1913, one of the first acts of the Alaskan territorial government was to grant women the right to vote. Seven years later, in 1920, the Nineteenth Amendment would finally grant this right to all women in the United States.

▲ Gold seekers often had to learn new skills, such as using dogsleds and navigating in the Arctic, when they came to the Yukon in the 1890s.

In 1910, James Wickersham wrote an article explaining why Alaska should become a state. He titled his plea "The Forty-ninth Star." As Alaska's delegate to the U.S. Congress, Wickersham introduced a statehood bill in 1916. The bill did not pass.

World War I had an unexpected effect on Alaska's statehood hopes. As Alaskan men joined the military, the population decreased. Fewer people made it harder for Alaska to meet the population requirements for statehood.

While some people worked to strengthen Alaska's role in the United States, others worked to protect its majestic lands. Charles Sheldon, a hunter and nature expert, was an energetic supporter of Alaska's wilderness. His passionate work led to the formation of Mount McKinley National Park in 1917. One year later, Katmai National Monument was established and in 1925, a significant portion of Glacier Bay was added to Alaska's protected parkland.

World War II

In December 1941, the United States entered war with Japan and Alaska's location became strategically important. The western regions of Alaska were the part of the United States nearest to Asia. U.S. military leaders feared invasion. At the time, no major highway joined Alaska with the other states. The military began an ambitious project: building the Alaskan-Canadian Highway. Stretching 1,522 miles (2,449 km) from Dawson Creek in the Canadian province of British Columbia to Fairbanks, the highway was completed in an amazing eight months. Workers put in twenty-hour days in temperatures of minus 40 degrees Fahrenheit (minus 40 degrees Celsius) to finish this vital roadway.

Rights for Native Alaskans

In 1913, men from many different cultures and groups joined together to form the Alaska Native Brotherhood. Two years later, the Alaska Native Sisterhood was founded. Together, these groups worked to gain and protect the rights of Alaska's Native peoples. In 1929, the groups tried to persuade Congress to recognize Native land claims. Although unsuccessful, this early effort laid the groundwork for the recognition of these rights in 1971's Alaska Native Claims Settlement Act.

The fears of invasion were justified. In June 1942, Japan attacked the Aleutian Islands. After heavy bombing, the Japanese troops invaded Kiska and Attu islands, the only parts of North America invaded during the war. In May 1943, more than thirty-four thousand U.S. troops regained control of Attu Island in a bloody battle. When the United States took control, many Japanese soldiers committed suicide rather than be captured. The United States finally regained Kiska by August after another series of attacks on the Japanese invaders.

▲ American troops regained Attu in 1943 during one of the most deadly battles of World War II. American casualties included 550 dead, 1,500 wounded, and 1,200 injured by the harsh, cold climate. Nearly all of the 2,500 Japanese occupiers died.

Statehood and Beyond

After World War II, the statehood movement gained momentum in Alaska. The Aleutian invasions emphasized the importance of the territory's location. Alaska's closeness to Russia drew attention to the area as tensions between the United States and Russia grew in the period of rivalry and suspicion known as the Cold War. However, yet another factor brought focus to Alaska: oil. When a large deposit was discovered on the Kenai Peninsula in 1957, people stopped seeing Alaska as a poor, dependent region. Alaska's natural resources made it seem like a potentially rich state.

Alaska became the forty-ninth state on January 3, 1959. William A. Egan was elected the first governor, and a spirit of hope and pride ran through the state. Since then, Alaskans have tried to balance growth with preservation, while recovering from some devastating disasters. On March 27, 1964, Anchorage was rocked by the largest earthquake ever to hit North America. Estimated to measure 9.2 on the Richter scale, the quake caused enormous damage, destroying many towns and ports in the Prince William Sound region. The quake also caused deadly tidal waves (tsunamis). Three years later, Fairbanks was deluged by record-breaking rains, leading to damaging and costly floods.

As these tragedies prove, Alaska's environment can be dangerous. However, it can also be a source of plenty. In 1968, the largest oil field in the United States was

Did You Know?

After the invasion of Attu, the United States government was worried about future attacks on Alaska. In the name of protection, it forced 881 Aleuts to leave their homes and live in abandoned buildings in southeastern Alaska. The conditions were crowded and unhealthy. Men left their families alone to hunt for seals. Sixteen Aleuts died. In 1988, the U.S. government officially apologized to the Aleuts and financially compensated them for the poor treatment they had received.

discovered at Prudhoe Bay. The Trans-Alaska Pipeline was completed in 1977 to carry oil 800 miles (1,287 km) south across the landscape to Valdez, so it can be transported by boat. The pipeline is so long that it takes oil nearly six days to travel from one end to the other. The discovery of oil led to an economic boom in Alaska. In 1976, Alaskan voters amended the state constitution to create the Alaska Permanent Fund. This state savings account allows all Alaskans to benefit from oil's profits. Every year, half of the earnings of this fund are distributed to eligible Alaskans.

Another disaster in 1989 emphasized the fragile balance between economic activity and the environment. The *Exxon Valdez*, an oil tanker, struck a reef, spilling eleven million gallons of crude oil into Prince William Sound. The pollution killed more than three hundred thousand sea birds, five thousand otters, and many other marine animals. The cleanup project was completed in 1992 at a cost of $2 billion.

Land Rights

In 1971, the Alaska Native Claims Settlement Act recognized the land rights of Alaska's Native peoples. The act granted $962 million and about forty-four million acres of land to Alaskan Native Americans. The act established twelve Native corporations to manage the money and land. Each corporation has made its own spending decisions. Some have handled the funds wisely and are thriving. Others have little money left, though they still hold their valuable land rights.

▼ A cleanup crew sprays chemicals on an Alaska beach in an effort to neutralize the effects of oil from the Exxon Valdez spill.

They Live in Alaska

> [I] tried to imagine the people who would choose to live in such a place. Alaska was, clearly, a land one would have to choose. Not a place one just happened to stumble across.
>
> — *Author Joe McGinnis,* Going to Extremes, *1980*

With plenty of room to grow, Alaska's population has increased rapidly in recent decades. Between 1960 and 2000, Alaska's population more than doubled, making it the fourth-fastest-growing population in the United States, after Nevada, Arizona, and Florida. However, the rate of growth has slowed in recent years. Between 1990 and 2000, the population grew by a rate of about 14 percent, only a little higher than the national average of 13.1 percent.

Only about 38 percent of Alaskans were born in the state. Many people who move there from other states or countries are attracted to the region's economic promise and dramatic environment. Some are hoping to escape the congestion of more populated regions. Many serve in the U.S. military at one of Alaska's many military bases. Others have moved to Alaska for jobs, particularly in the oil industry.

Age Distribution in Alaska
(2000 Census)

Age	Population
0–4	47,591
5–19	160,526
20–24	39,892
25–44	203,522
45–64	139,702
65 & over	35,699

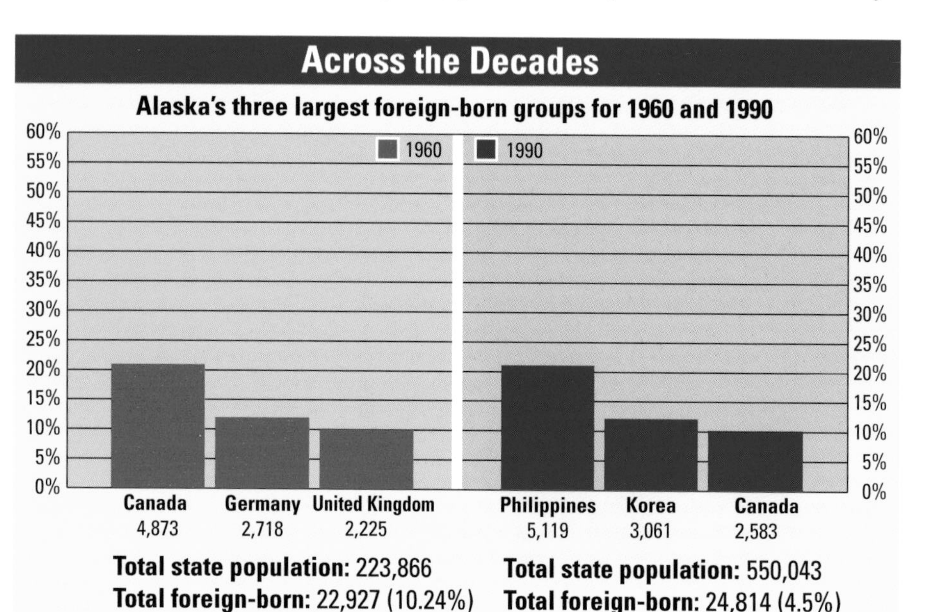

Patterns of Immigration

The total number of people who immigrated to Alaska in 1998 was 1,008. Of that number, the largest groups were from the Philippines (24%), Mexico (10%), and Russia (9%).

Population growth is not even throughout Alaska. Urban populations are growing much faster than those in rural areas. About two-thirds of Alaskans live in cities. In fact, more than 40 percent of Alaskans live in Anchorage. Rural communities in Alaska include tiny villages and communities in the Arctic tundra as well as small coastal villages in the Aleutian Islands. Although many of these regions are far from urban centers, many residents use telephone or Internet connections for communicating.

▲ Eskimo dancers celebrate a uniquely Native American Fourth of July.

Ethnicities

Native Americans are by far the largest nonwhite ethnic group in Alaska. Descendants of the first people to live in the region, this group represents almost 16 percent of the population, a far greater percentage than any other state. Native Alaskans, including the Inuit who live in northern and western Alaska, and the Aleut of the Alaskan Peninsula and the Aleutian Islands represent about two-thirds of this group. About one-third of this group identify themselves as Native Americans, including the Tlingit, Haida, and Athabascan.

Did You Know?

Peter Kalifornsky, born on the Kenai Peninsula in 1911, is the last living speaker of his Athabascan dialect. He worked with researchers at the University of Alaska to create a record of this vanishing language.

Heritage and Background, Alaska **Year 2000**

▶ Here is a look at the racial background of Alaska today. Alaska ranks thirty-fourth among all U.S. states with regard to African Americans as a percentage of the population.

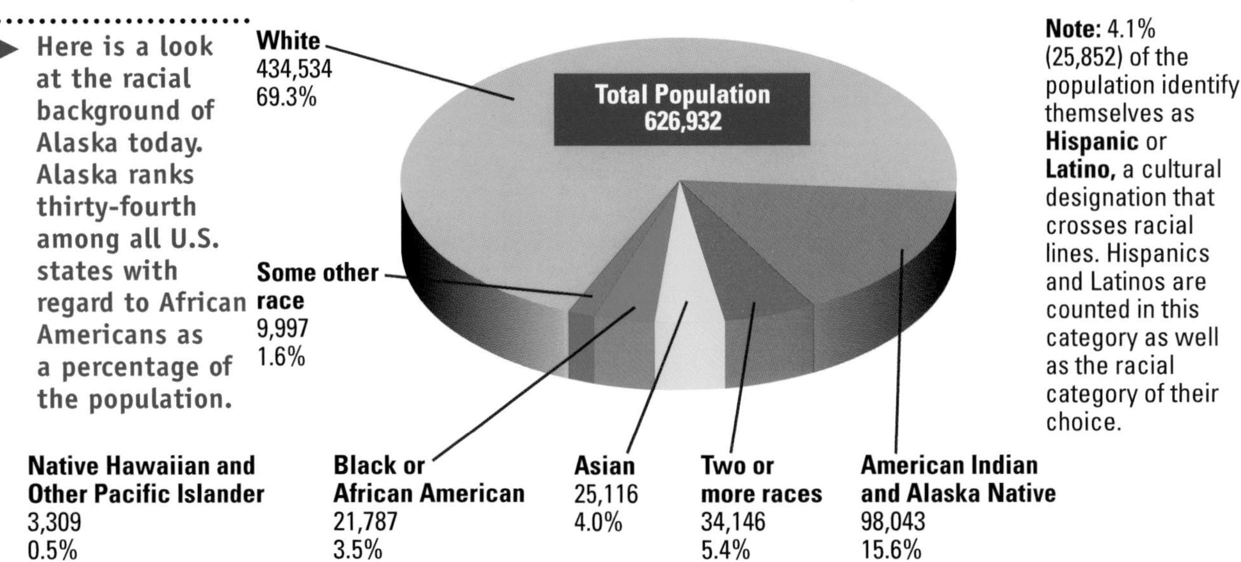

Note: 4.1% (25,852) of the population identify themselves as **Hispanic** or **Latino,** a cultural designation that crosses racial lines. Hispanics and Latinos are counted in this category as well as the racial category of their choice.

Today, most Alaskan Natives belong to one of twelve Native corporations established in 1971. These corporations include members from more than two hundred individual villages and cooperatives. The Native corporations manage the land and money owned by each regional group and also protect the rights of their members.

Geography plays a key role in Alaska's immigration patterns. Many people who move to Alaska come from its neighboring regions, such as Canada and Russia, as well as from the western states. Others cross the Pacific Ocean from Japan, Korea, Taiwan, the Philippines, and other countries of Asia. Still others come from countries that are farther away, but share similar climates.

Educational Levels of Alaska Workers (age 25 and over)	
Less than 9th grade	15,663
9th to 12th grade, no diploma	28,619
High school graduate, including equivalency	105,812
Some college, no degree or associate degree	135,655
Bachelor's degree	61,196
Graduate or professional degree	32,611

▼ A cable car brings riders to a breathtaking mountaintop view of Juneau, Alaska's capital.

Religion

▲ Fairbanks is home to one of three major campuses of the University of Alaska.

The first religions practiced in Alaska were those of Alaskan Natives. Each indigenous group incorporated religious beliefs in its cultural and social activities. For example, the Inupiaq and Yupik believe that spirits are recycled or reincarnated. Spirits can be both humans and animals. Formal rituals are followed in order to release the spirit from animals slaughtered for food or other uses. The Aleut begin their winter festivals with spiritual ceremonies that express their gladness for the bounty of the season and their hope for the future. Today, nearly 16 percent of Alaskans practice Native religions.

Since the first European settlers in Alaska were the Russians, Russian Orthodox churches were established in Kodiak and Sitka. A community on the Kenai Peninsula follows the traditional Russian Orthodox lifestyle, including dress, periods of fasting, and a strong focus on the study of holy books.

Later settlers brought other religions, and now churches and temples of nearly every faith are found in Alaska. About one-third of the population is affiliated with a Christian church and nearly 10 percent of the state's people are Catholic. Religious groups include Alaskan Moravian, Baha'i, Baptist, Christian Scientist, Episcopalian, Lutheran, Methodist, Mormon, and Presbyterian.

Education

Alaska's commitment to education is reflected in the state's 93.3 percent high school graduation rate — one of the highest in the United States. Many Alaskan schools combine strong traditional methods with modern technology. Alaska's schools also have one of the highest ratios of students to computers: five students for every Internet computer in the system.

There are three colleges in Alaska. The University of Alaska has campuses throughout the state, reaching students in both urban and rural communities. Students can also pursue degrees at Sheldon Jackson College in Sitka or Alaska Pacific University in Anchorage.

Unique State, Unique Schools

Many students who attend the University of Alaska choose coursework that is uniquely Alaskan. In addition to earning degrees in marine biology, environmental science, or petroleum technology, students might choose to minor in Alaska Native studies or aviation technology. Classes with a strong Alaskan accent include Geology of Ore Deposits, Arctic Engineering, and Dog Mushing.

Variety and Icy Spectacle

> In the evening, after witnessing the unveiling of the majestic peaks and glaciers . . . it seemed inconceivable that nature could have anything finer to show us. Nevertheless, compared with what was to come the next morning, all that was as nothing.
>
> — *Naturalist John Muir describing his first views of Glacier Bay in 1879, from* Travels in Alaska *(1914)*

Alaska is by far the largest state (in land area) in the United States. Its total land area is 571,951 square miles (1,481,353 sq km). Geologists divide this huge area into four natural regions: the Pacific Mountain System, the Central Uplands and Lowlands, the Rocky Mountain System, and the Arctic Coastal Plain.

Highest Point
Mount McKinley
20,320 feet (6,194 m) above sea level

The Pacific Mountain System

The Pacific Mountain System covers much of the western coast of the United States, arching from the Aleutian Islands in the far west along south-central Alaska and the coast in the southeast. The mountain system continues along the coast into southern California.

Alaska's panhandle is the part of the state's coastal land that extends to the southeast. Varying from 10 to 150 miles in width (16 to 241 km), the panhandle includes mountains, ice fields, and narrow inlets between cliffs, called fjords. Two mountain ranges lie northwest of the panhandle: the Saint

▼ *From left to right:* sled dogs in Denali National Park; ice climbers ascend a steep glacier wall in the Alaska Range; visitors pan for gold at the Independence Mine State Historical Park in the Talkeetna Mountains; Ketchikan Totem Park; caribou; an Alaskan whale watch.

Elias Range and the Wrangell Mountains. The Talkeetna Mountains and the Alaska Range are located farther inland.

The Alaska Peninsula and the Aleutian Islands are in the southwestern part of the state. The Aleutian Range, which runs along the center of both regions, includes many active volcanoes.

The Copper River Basin and Susitna-Cook Inlet are lowland areas within the Pacific Mountain System. Both areas are forested lowland, but also contain some of Alaska's most fertile farmland.

Average January temperature
Anchorage:
14.9°F (–9.5°C)
Fairbanks:
–10.1°F (–23.4°C)

Average July temperature
Anchorage:
58.4°F (14.7°C)
Fairbanks:
62.4°F (16.9°C)

Average yearly rainfall
Anchorage:
15.91 inches (40.41 cm)
Fairbanks:
10.87 inches (27.6 cm)

Average yearly snowfall
Anchorage:
69.5 inches (176.5 cm)
Fairbanks:
70.1 inches (178.1 cm)

The Central Uplands and Lowlands

The largest land region in Alaska, the Central Uplands and Lowlands, is sandwiched between the Alaska Range in the south and the Brooks Range in the north. The region's hills and swampy river valley roll from the Canadian border in the east to the Seward Peninsula in the west. The highlands include the Kuskokwim Mountains, while the lowlands include muskeg — soggy material that covers the earth like a wet blanket. It is made up of dead plant material, particularly moss. Muskeg, also called peat bog, covers about 10 percent of southeastern Alaska.

The Rocky Mountain System

The Rocky Mountains of the lower United States extend through Canada into Alaska, where they include the peaks of the Brooks Range. These steep mountains of northern Alaska were carved by glaciers that moved through the region thousands of years ago. Mountains eroded by glaciers typically show sharp or jagged profiles.

Largest Lakes

Iliamna Lake
640,000 acres
(259,008 hectares)

Becharof Lake
293,120 acres
(118,626 ha)

Teshekpuk Lake
201,600 acres
(81,588 ha)

The Arctic Coastal Plain

Extending north from the Rocky Mountain System, the Arctic Coastal Plain is Alaska's northernmost region. The

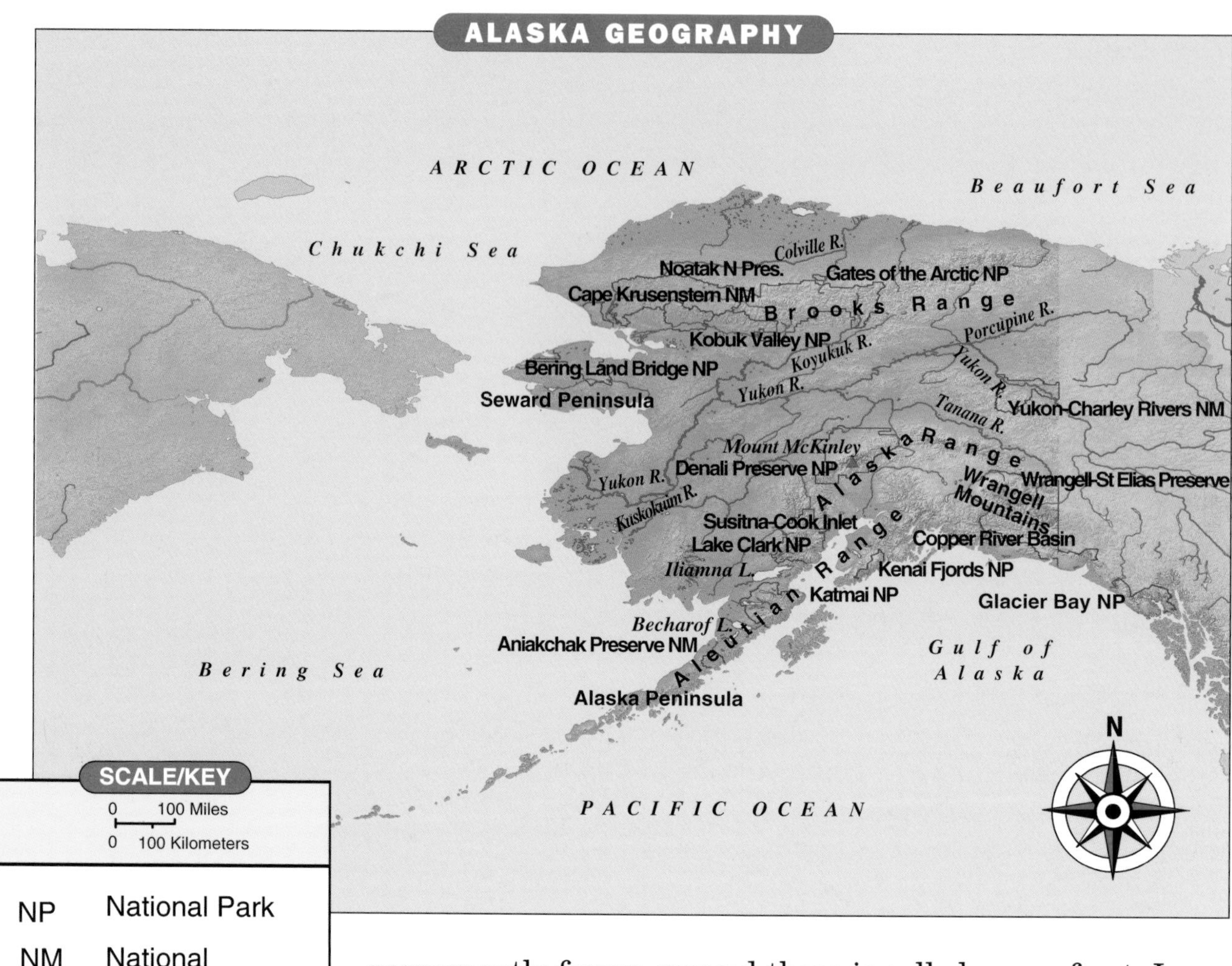

permanently frozen ground there is called permafrost. In the summer, tundra develops as the upper surface thaws, allowing plants such as grasses and wildflowers to grow.

Plants and Animals

One-third of Alaska is forested, although relatively few varieties of trees can grow in the state's challenging climate. The state tree, the Sitka spruce, grows in coastal forests, as does the western hemlock. White spruces, lodgepole pines, paper birches, and black cottonwoods grow in other regions.

Brilliant wildflowers bloom during a short season. Bright purple pasque flowers signal the beginning of the flower season in late May. During the next three months, blooms include bearberries, fireweed, forget-me-nots, arctic poppies, and lowbush cranberries.

Alaska is home to a huge variety of large wild animals. Bears found in Alaska include brown and black bears, grizzlies, and polar bears. Migrating caribou travel more than

1,000 miles (1,609 km) every year. Dall sheep, with their majestic curved horns, run gracefully atop jagged cliffs. Other mammals include wolves, elk, beavers, foxes, and musk oxen.

Residents and tourists who gaze skyward may be lucky enough to spot one of the state's more than four hundred native birds. More bald eagles live in Alaska than in the other states combined. Arctic terns migrate farther than any other bird. With just a little patience, Alaskan birdwatchers can also spot loons, whimbrels, golden plovers, long-tailed jaegers, snow buntings, goshawks, cormorants, and puffins.

The shores, lakes, and deep waters of Alaska are habitats for thousands of animals, including sea lions, seals, sea otters, walruses, porpoises, and whales. The government places restrictions on or outlaws the hunting of many of these animals. Playful sea otters use primitive tools, banging rocks on shellfish to crack them open. Whale watches offer a safe method for viewing some of Alaska's marine animals.

Major Rivers

Yukon River
1,979 miles (3,184 km)

Kuskokwim River
724 miles (1,165 km)

Tanana River
659 miles (1,060 km)

▼ Denali National Park highlights the rugged peaks of the Alaska Range.

Oil, Fish, and the Future

> Alaska must be allowed to be Alaska, that is her greatest economy. I hope the United States of America is not so rich that she can afford to let these wildernesses pass by, or so poor she cannot afford to keep them.
>
> — *Conservationist Margaret Murie, speaking in favor of the Alaska Lands Act in September 1964*

The Alaskan economy is tied directly to the land. Many people work to make use of Alaska's key natural resources, including oil and minerals. However, the greatest percentage of people work in public service. Government employees work at the federal, state, and local levels. They also include men and women working at the state's forty-five military bases or offices.

One of the key factors affecting Alaska's economy is its remote location. Even though some natural resources are plentiful, it can be very costly to transport these resources outside the state. Other states often experience rapid economic growth because their resources are located near the places where they are sold — the markets. Alaska's resources are usually located far from their markets. Labor costs are also relatively high. Many employers need to pay skilled workers higher-than-average salaries in order to encourage them to relocate to Alaska.

Top Employers
(of workers age sixteen and over)

Sector	Percent
Services	43.5%
Wholesale and retail trade	14.2%
Federal, state, and local government (including military)	10.7%
Transportation, communications, and public utilities	11.6%
Construction	7.3%
Agriculture, forestry, fisheries, and mining	4.9%
Finance, insurance, and real estate	4.6%
Manufacturing	3.3%

Agriculture, Forestry, and Mining

Relatively little of Alaska's land is used for farming. It is often cheaper for Alaskans to buy foods grown in the south and shipped to the state. However, Alaska does boast unusually large summer crops. Vegetables grow far larger in Alaska than they would farther south because of the twenty-four hours of sunlight every day during the peak growing season. It isn't unusual to find ninety-pound cabbages and fifteen-pound carrots.

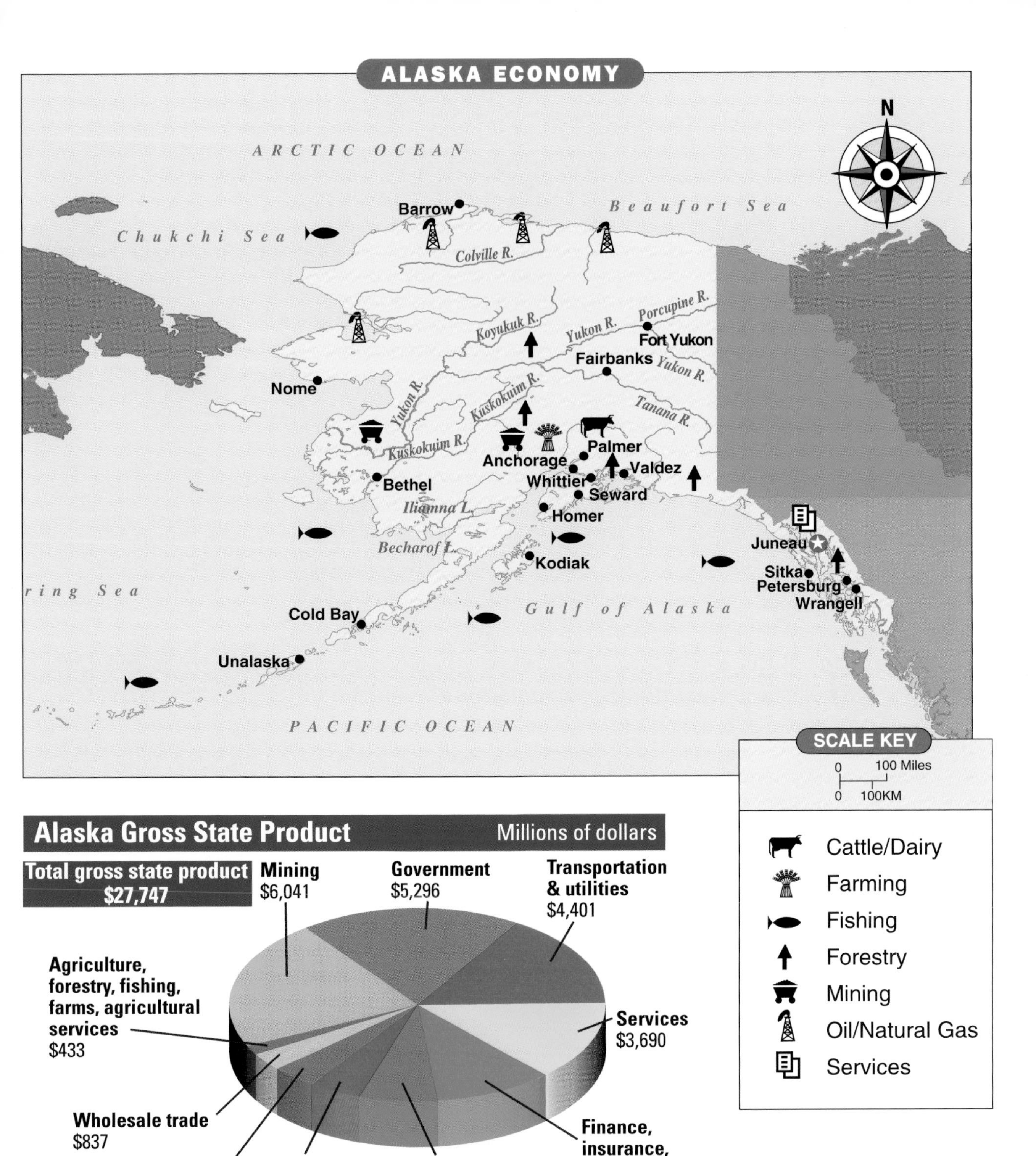

ALASKA ECONOMY
N
ARCTIC OCEAN
Chukchi Sea
Beaufort Sea
Barrow
Colville R.
Koyukuk R.
Yukon R.
Porcupine R.
Fort Yukon
Fairbanks
Yukon R.
Nome
Yukon R.
Kuskokwim R.
Tanana R.
Kuskokwim R.
Palmer
Anchorage
Valdez
Whittier
Seward
Bethel
Iliamna L.
Homer
Becharof L.
Kodiak
Juneau
Sitka
Petersburg
Wrangell
ring Sea
Gulf of Alaska
Cold Bay
Unalaska
PACIFIC OCEAN
SCALE KEY
0 100 Miles
0 100KM
Cattle/Dairy
Farming
Fishing
Forestry
Mining
Oil/Natural Gas
Services
Alaska Gross State Product
Millions of dollars
Total gross state product $27,747
Mining $6,041
Government $5,296
Transportation & utilities $4,401
Services $3,690
Finance, insurance, & real estate $2,852
Retail trade $1,858
Construction $1,266
Manufacturing $1,073
Wholesale trade $837
Agriculture, forestry, fishing, farms, agricultural services $433

Although land in Alaska is rarely used to produce food, water is a major source of revenue. Fishing is a key Alaskan industry. More fish are harvested in Alaska than in any other state, and fisheries employ more people than other private companies. Fish produced in Alaska include salmon, cod, ocean perch, halibut, and herring. Dungeness crabs are also harvested in offshore waters. Overfishing, however, has led to serious decreases in fish populations. The Magneson Act, passed in 1976, protects waters up to 200 miles (322 km) from the Alaskan coast. This law limits the numbers of fish that can be caught, ensuring there will be enough for future use.

▲ Fisheries preserve freshly caught fish so it can be shipped around the world. Pelican Seafoods, a division of Kake Tribal Corporation, in Pelican is a buying and processing service for local fishers.

Oil and natural gas are the state's most valuable resources and critical to Alaska's economy. When oil prices are high, the economy booms. Low prices can mean difficult times. Most of the oil in Alaska comes from the North Slope oil field near Prudhoe Bay. Several hundred workers operate the industrial facility at Prudhoe Bay. Working twelve-hour days, these employees harness the vast underground oil and gas reserves. However, because the oil reserves are limited, economists are looking for other ways to boost Alaska's growth. Some people want to build another pipeline to tap the huge natural gas reserves in the North Slope. Alaskans also collect other minerals from the land, including gold, sand, gravel, silver, zinc, and coal.

Manufacturing

The goods manufactured in Alaska begin with the state's natural resources. Some factories produce food products for export. Processed seafood represents the greatest percentage of Alaska's food production. Factories use a variety of techniques to preserve fresh fish so it can be enjoyed throughout the world, producing everything from canned salmon and smoked herring to salted roe and frozen halibut. Timber from the forests of the southeast is manufactured into wood products, including logs, lumber, paper, and pulp. Animal furs and pelts are another source of revenue for Alaskan manufacturers.

Fish Farms and Fish Ranchers

Some fish can be grown on farms, but not Alaska's famous salmon. In order to protect the quality and health of the salmon population, the state does not allow salmon farming. Although it isn't legal to raise salmon in pens, fish "ranchers" are allowed to raise young salmon in hatcheries. These young fish are then released into the wild, where they boost the salmon population. Unlike salmon, shellfish can be legally raised in farms. Alaskan farmers raise Pacific oysters, blue mussels, littleneck clams, and scallops in underwater hatcheries. Most of these crops take from one and a half to three years to reach maturity.

Transportation, Services, and Tourism

▲ Cruises are a popular way to see Alaska's natural beauty. Tour boats offer exciting views, but also help to prevent damage to fragile wilderness areas by limiting human contact with animals and land resources.

Unlike most states, roads in Alaska are few and far between. Instead, major transportation routes are on water and in the air. In fact, Alaska has issued more private pilot's licenses than any other state. Bush pilots specialize in landing their small planes in regions that are difficult to reach in any other way. Major airports in Alaska include those in Anchorage and Fairbanks. In addition to providing a major hub for tourists, the Anchorage airport is an important refueling station for planes using the polar route to travel between Europe, Asia, and North America.

Service industries employ many of the state's workers. In addition to the large number of people working for the government, service industries include those who work in restaurants, stores, and real estate and insurance sales. Tourism is a vital part of the service industry in Alaska. Millions of people from around the world visit Alaska every year. Local residents offer their help as tour guides, hotel keepers, and boat captains. Alaskan tourism includes a wide range of experiences. Visitors can ride anything from cruise ships and kayaks to trains, planes, and even dogsleds. After visiting a dogsled kennel operated by a former Iditarod participant, a tourist can take a private airplane tour led by a bush pilot flying into untouched, remote regions.

A growing trend is ecotourism, also known as low-impact tourism. Cruises are a popular way to see Alaska's natural beauty. Tour boats offer exciting views that cannot be seen from Alaska's interior. Ecotourists show that they value and respect the natural wonders they are visiting. Their care and concern helps ensure that these magnificent sights will be available for others to enjoy in the future.

Major Airports

Airport	Location	Passengers per year (2000)
Anchorage International	Anchorage	5,030,557
Fairbanks International	Fairbanks	855,908

Made in Alaska

Leading farm products and crops
Salmon
Other fish
Shellfish
Beef
Barley
Oats
Hay
Potatoes
Lettuce

Other products
Petroleum products
Wood products
Furs

Balance of Powers

> Fellow Alaskans, the state of our state is strong. Our source of strength is citizenship and unity.
>
> *– Governor Tony Knowles in his State of the State address, January 16, 2002*

The Alaskan constitution was adopted in 1956. Citizens of the region hoped that adopting the constitution would help them gain statehood. The National Municipal League called the constitution "one of the best, if not the best state constitution ever written." Three years later, the territory of Alaska became the forty-ninth state of the United States.

Like the Constitution of the United States, Alaska's constitution is a flexible document, but amendments must follow a strict process. First, two-thirds of the voters in both houses of the state legislature must approve of the proposed amendment. Then the people of the state make the final decision. In order to become a permanent constitutional amendment, two-thirds of the voters must also approve the change.

The government in Alaska is similar in many ways to the government of the United States. Based on its constitution, the state government provides the laws and leadership to protect the state's citizens. It has three branches: executive, legislative, and judicial. The executive branch administers laws, the legislative branch makes laws, and the judicial branch interprets laws.

Native corporations also play a crucial role in Alaskan government. These corporations were established to allow Native Americans to work with the local and state governments to protect their rights and interests.

The Executive Branch

The governor of Alaska is the state's chief executive. Voters elect the governor and lieutenant governor to four-year terms.

State Constitution

We the people of Alaska, grateful to God and to those who founded our nation and pioneered this great land, in order to secure and transmit to succeeding generations our heritage of political, civil, and religious liberty within the Union of States, do ordain and establish this constitution for the State of Alaska.

— Preamble to the 1956 Alaska State Constitution

Elected Posts in the Executive Branch		
Office	**Length of Term**	**Term Limits**
Governor	4 years	2 consecutive terms
Lieutenant Governor	4 years	2 consecutive terms
Attorney General	unlimited	none
Superintendent of Schools	unlimited	none
Commissioner of Labor	unlimited	none

Did You Know?

The governor's mansion in Juneau is just nine blocks away from a habitat where grizzly bears live. The mansion was the first structure built for the territorial government.

The Alaskan constitution gives the governor the power to direct the budget, deciding how state money is collected and distributed. Another executive power is the right to veto proposed legislation.

The governor also influences statewide office by appointing people to administer many state departments. The fourteen state departments are Administration, Community and Regional Affairs, Commerce and Economic Development, Corrections, Education, Environmental Conservation, Fish and Game, Health and Social Services, Labor, Law, Military and Veterans Affairs, Natural Resources, Public Safety, Revenue, and Transportation and Public Facilities.

The Legislative Branch

Alaska's legislative branch includes a Senate and a House of Representatives. There are twenty senatorial districts, each of which elects one senator. Each of the forty representative districts elects a representative. Because Alaska's population changes, election districts are modified every ten years based on the most recent census data.

The legislature meets for no more than 120 days each year, beginning on the third Monday in January. Although the constitution places this time limit on legislative sessions, the governor or the legislature itself may call for a ten-day extension or a special thirty-day session.

▼ Completed in 1931, the State Capitol is home to the Alaska House and Senate when they are in session.

The Judicial Branch

The judicial branch of the Alaskan government is divided into four courts. The state supreme court is the highest court in Alaska. Five justices appointed by the governor sit on the court, which hears appeals of cases from the lower courts. Below the supreme court is the court of appeals. This three-member judicial panel was created in 1980 to focus on appeals in criminal cases.

The superior court is the general trial court for the state. There are thirty-two superior court judges with court locations throughout the state. Superior courts hear both civil and criminal cases. Each of Alaska's four judicial districts has a district court. While most cases are heard in the superior court, district courts hear limited cases, including some small claims and domestic violence cases.

All courts are managed by the state. There are no city or municipal courts, although tribal courts operate at a village level. These courts often address Indian Child Welfare Act cases as well as some adoptions. Tribal courts or village councils also hear cases involving local disturbances such as disorderly conduct or juvenile offenses. They have the power to impose fines or require community service.

Local Government

At the local level, Alaska's government includes borough administrators, city officials, and representatives from Native corporations. Administrators help to govern each of Alaska's twelve boroughs. City councils operate in Alaska's largest towns and cities. Because much of the state's population is located in major cities such as Anchorage and Fairbanks, the mayors of these cities have substational power to change their city and state.

One unique aspect of Alaska's government is the input provided by the twelve Native corporations. Established by the Alaska Native Claims Settlement Act of 1971, these corporations help Native Alaskans protect their land rights. Today, the twelve corporations work with the state

Legislature

House	Number of Members	Length of Term	Term Limits
Senate	20 senators	4 years	none
House of Representatives	40 representatives	2 years	none

government to make sure that all people in Alaska are governed fairly. The twelve native corporations include representatives of more than 120 tribes and villages.

National Representation

Like all states, Alaska has two senators in the U.S. Senate. Because of its small population, Alaska has only one representative in the U.S. House of Representatives. The state holds three Electoral College votes.

Alaska Politics

In addition to the traditional Democratic and Republican parties, Alaska has seen the growth of several "third parties." Alaska was the first state in which the Green Party, which focuses on environmental issues, was given a place on an election ballot. The Libertarian Party, which promotes limits on the role of government, has also gained support.

Alaskan politics shift with the important issues of the times. As economic challenges increase, voters look for leaders who will help the state grow and change. Political parties often support specific agendas. Some politicians favor development of all natural resources, such as the huge natural gas deposits in Prudhoe Bay. Others favor protecting the environment and the rights of Native Americans, both of which could be damaged by this development. Also, the push to open the Arctic National Wildlife Refuge to oil development is very controversial.

▼ **The William A. Egan Civic & Convention Center in Anchorage is a modern meeting hall for many events.**

Alaska's First Governor

When Alaska became a state in 1959, the citizens elected William A. Egan as their first state governor. Egan was born in Valdez, and his lifelong commitment to guiding the new state impressed voters. His personal style combined strength and firmness with fairness and good humor.

Before entering politics, Egan held many different jobs. His experiences as a truck driver, gold miner, fisherman, and pilot reflect many of Alaska's most important industries and services. After serving in the army air corps during World War II, Egan opened a general store in Valdez. Soon he joined the territorial government as a member of the house of representatives and later the senate.

Egan served three terms as governor. Every year on October 8, the state officially celebrates William A. Egan Day to honor his "lifetime of service to the territory and state of Alaska."

Traditions in New Alaska

And yet, there is only / One great thing, The only thing: / To live to see in huts and on journeys / The great day that dawns And the light that fills the world.

— from a traditional song of the Kitlinguiharmiut, recorded and translated by Knud Rasmussen, in **The Report of the Fifth Thule Expedition, 1921–1924: The Danish Expedition to Arctic North America**

A wide variety of cultures exist throughout the vast state of Alaska. Some native Alaskans follow traditional lifestyles in small, remote villages; urban newcomers enjoy the opportunities and setting of modern Anchorage. One of the distinct features of Alaskan life is that people can enjoy aspects of many different cultures and lifestyles. Some remote, traditional villages are now connected to the Internet, while city dwellers in Anchorage are only a short drive away from spectacular natural beauty.

The indigenous people of Alaska have distinct cultures, each group possessing a long and rich heritage. Many Native Alaskans make their living by subsistence farming or fishing, depending on the food they raise or catch themselves. Natives along the southern coast spend the summer hunting deer and catching salmon and other fish. Properly prepared and stored, these foods help them survive the long Alaskan winter. The Athabascans, who live in Alaska's interior, fish in the rivers and hunt caribou. Eskimos living in northern Alaska hunt seals and whale.

The development of native corporations has affected the cultural and economic life of most Native Alaskans. Although the corporations

DID YOU KNOW?

Barrow, Alaska, is the northernmost point of the United States. Once an Eskimo village, Barrow rapidly modernized when oil was discovered at Prudhoe Bay.

▼ A touring car from 1937 parked in the gold rush town of Skagway, beside the 1899 Arctic Brotherhood Hall.

have not been equally successful, many of these have created great wealth out of the land granted to them by the 1971 Alaska Native Claims Settlement Act. This wealth has led to some changes in traditional ways. Many sled dog teams have been replaced by modern vehicles. Motorboats have replaced traditional boats made of seal skin.

Descendants of the first Russians to arrive in Alaska live in Kodiak, Sitka, and the Kenai Peninsula. Kodiak and Sitka reflect a strong Russian cultural and religious heritage. Many members of Alaska's Russian Orthodox communities follow traditional styles of dress.

Many of Alaska's traditions and celebrations relate to the seasons and climate. Most of the rivers in the interior freeze during winter. "Breakup" is the name given to the time when the ice breaks up, marking the beginning of summer. In Nenana, it has been a tradition since 1917 to bet on the exact date and time that ice on the Tanana River will break.

During winter festivals, Alaskans gather to celebrate their communities. The winter fun begins in December at the Barrow Winter Games. In January, Kodiak celebrates Russian New Year. By January, the long, dark days have begun to sap people's spirits. Winter carnivals like the Anchorage Fur Rendezvous, Wrangell Tent City Winter Festival, Cordova Ice Worm Festival, and the Valdez

The Northern Lights

Alaska is the best place in the United States to view the northern lights. These spectacular lights in the sky, also known as the Aurora Borealis, are the result of charged particles from the Sun hitting Earth's magnetic field. The northern lights are best viewed in winter when it is very dark. Native Alaskans have many legends about these astonishing and sometimes unsettling lights. One legend describes the aurora as people playing a game like football in the sky, only with a walrus head for a ball. Another legend claims that the aurora can howl, whistle, and crackle. Some superstitions recommend carrying a knife as protection against the mystical dangers of the northern lights.

International Ice Climbing Festival brighten up many dark winter days.

Another popular winter activity is viewing the northern lights. Although they are visible in Anchorage, the lights are usually more dramatic farther north. Many people in Anchorage take a night drive at least once each winter, heading north in hope of seeing Alaska's natural fireworks.

▲ **Performers bring Alaskan legends to life at the Soapy Smith Days musical theater in Skagway.**

Libraries and Museums

The Alaska State Library is located in Juneau. The collection includes a rich variety of books, magazines, historical documents, and state archives. The library also manages an online image bank that allows Internet users around the world to visit Alaska without leaving home. The University of Alaska has major libraries on its campuses in Fairbanks, Anchorage, and Juneau. Public libraries also operate in most of Alaska's cities.

The Alaska State Museum is also located in the capital city of Juneau. This museum has permanent exhibits dedicated to Alaska's Native people, the natural history of the region, its Russian heritage, and its modern history.

DID YOU KNOW?

The oldest museum in Alaska is the Sheldon Jackson Museum in Sitka. It is named for Rev. Dr. Sheldon Jackson, who contributed Native artifacts collected while traveling in Alaska. The museum was founded in 1887 and soon outgrew its home. Its current home, and first concrete building in the state, opened ten years later. It exhibits everything from full-size kayaks and totems to an assortment of traditional jewelry and toys.

Other museums in the state of Alaska focus on specific histories, cultures, or eras. Artifacts of the early days of plane travel in Alaska and historic aviation videos are featured at the Alaska Aviation Heritage Museum in Anchorage. In Anchorage, tourists enjoy the Alaska Native Heritage Center, the Anchorage Museum of History and Art, and the Elmendorf Museum, which features wildlife and ecosystem displays. The Dog Mushing Museum in Fairbanks highlights this traditional form of transportation.

Museums dedicated to the cultures and arts of Native Alaskans include the Inupiat Heritage Center in Barrow, Huslia Cultural Center in Huslia, the Totem Heritage Center in Ketchikan, and the Museum of the Aleutians in Unalaska. Other popular museums document key historic events or resources. The Klondike Gold Rush National Historical Park in Skagway includes over two hundred thousand artifacts from the Klondike Gold Rush.

DID YOU KNOW?

Alaskans have jumped onto the Internet in record numbers. About 69 percent of all adults have access to the Internet — a greater percentage of the population than in any other state.

Communications

Alaska's huge size and rugged land make communications difficult but important. Newspapers, radio broadcasts, and television programs carry essential information such as

▼ The Alaska State Museum in Juneau includes displays that highlight native Alaskan cultures.

▶ A dog team pulls through the icy course at the World Champion Sled Race.

weather and hunting reports throughout the state.

In 1868, the *Sitka Times* became Alaska's first newspaper. Today, several daily newspapers are published in Alaska, including the *Anchorage Daily News,* the *Fairbanks Daily News-Miner*, the *Juneau Empire*, the *Ketchikan Daily News,* and the *Kodiak Daily Mirror*. Rural communities are served by local papers such as the *Tundra Drums,* the *Seward Phoenix Log,* and the *Valdez Vanguard*. Many newspapers operate Internet sites that spread news and resources to a wider audience.

Radio and television are also key sources of information throughout the state. More than sixty local AM or FM radio stations broadcast news, bulletins, music, and more. The first local television stations were launched in Anchorage in 1953. Today there are six stations broadcasting television programs from Anchorage, as well as stations in Fairbanks, Juneau, North Pole, and Sitka.

Music and Theater

Alaskans and visitors can enjoy a wide variety of music and theater, from traditional folk and Native music festivals and performances to popular singers and musicians on tour. On one night in Anchorage, music lovers might choose between jazz, classical, Latin, rock, and folk concerts. Poetry slams — entertaining competitions between poets who read their works aloud — are popular in Anchorage.

Much of Alaska's theater takes place in Anchorage, where playgoers get a chance to see many musical or dramatic productions. New works are showcased during the yearly Last Frontier Theater Conference in Valdez.

Sports

Alaskans play many of the same sports played in the "lower forty-eight," such as basketball, hockey, and baseball.

DID YOU KNOW?

As in other sports, there are specific positions in a sled dog team. The dogs at the front of the team are called the lead dogs. They move the team left or right when the musher gives the signal. These dogs need to be intelligent, quick, and alert. The swing dogs run just behind the lead dogs. They help set the pace and turn the team. Next come the team dogs, who give the team more power. Finally, the wheel dogs run next to the sled. They help steer the sled itself. During a race, mushers usually rotate dogs among several positions.

However, few other states feature a famous midnight baseball game, made possible by twenty-four hours of daylight during the peak of summer. Each June, the Midnight Sun Baseball Classic is held in Fairbanks. Play begins at 11:00 P.M. and goes well into the night.

The most famous sport in Alaska takes unique advantage of the climate and environment. Dog mushing is both the state sport and a tribute to an important traditional form of transportation. Dog mushing is another name for sled dog racing. During winter months, there are races throughout the state, but the most famous is the Iditarod Trail Sled Dog Race. Following historic routes traveled by dog teams that used to deliver the mail, this race has been popular since it first began in 1967. Expanded to its current length in 1973, the Iditarod course runs 1,050 miles (1,689 km) from Anchorage to Nome. Safety rules ensure the dogs get enough rest between the difficult stages of this remarkable journey, which often takes more than ten days to complete. Dogs used in mushing are usually Siberian huskies or Alaskan malamutes. Their thick fur helps them stay warm in the coldest weather. Special boots protect the dogs' paws from the icy trail.

Other winter sports played throughout Alaska include skiing, skating, bobsledding, and snowboarding. Wilderness hiking is popular with both visitors and residents. With fifteen national parks and many more recreation areas and trails, Alaska offers year-round challenges at every level, from a pleasant stroll in the volcanic landscape of Katmai National Park to an ambitious climb up Mount McKinley in Denali National Park.

For a faster tour of wintry landscapes, some Alaskans enjoy snowmobiling. These powerful machines are often used as work vehicles. Off-duty, they roll over rugged snowmobiling trails in many state parks. Snowmobile races are a popular spectator sport.

▶ Cleveland Cavalier's Trajan Langdon (21) races past Jud Buechler (30) of the Detroit Pistons.

Alaska Greats

Libby Riddles was the first woman to win the Iditarod. In 1985, she and her team of dogs faced a dangerous blizzard. Instead of waiting for the storm to pass, twenty-eight-year-old Riddles decided to leave Shaktoolik and keep going. This courageous move gave her team an unbeatable lead. Because of her memorable accomplishment in the race, the Women's Sports Foundation named her Professional Sportswoman of the Year.

Trajan Langdon plays basketball for the NBA's Cleveland Cavaliers. He started his career as a high school player in Anchorage. There he was named the Alaska Player of the Year three times and set an Alaskan AAAA-level record of scoring 2,200 career points. After a stellar college career at Duke, this Alaskan native was snapped up by Cleveland's talent scouts during the first round of the 1999 draft.

Great Alaskans

This was a wonderful place to grow up. We were isolated, I suppose, but we didn't know that there was an entirely different world out there beyond the mountains.

– Roberta Fraser Johnson, recalling her childhood in Treadwell, a now-disappeared company mining town on Douglas Island. From "Alaska's Gold Rush" by Stanton H. Patty, 1980

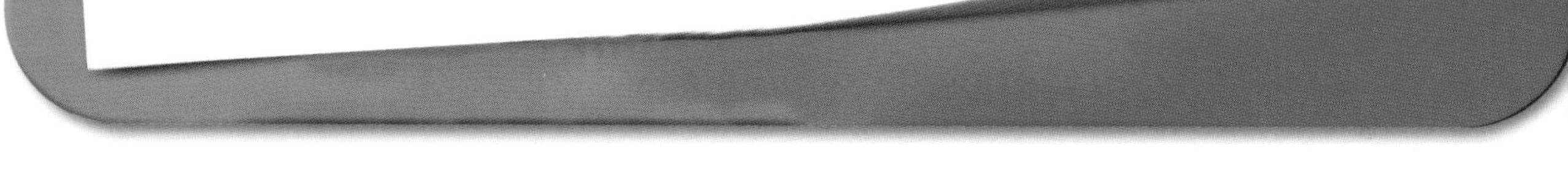

Following are only a few of the thousands of people who were born, died, or spent much of their lives in Alaska and made extraordinary contributions to the state and the nation.

VITUS JONASSEN BERING

EXPLORER

BORN: *1681, Horsens, Denmark*
DIED: *December 19, 1741, Bering Island*

Vitus Bering was an ambitious explorer. Born in Denmark, he enlisted in the Russian navy in 1703. For the rest of his life, he served Russia, returning only once to Denmark in 1715. On his first journey from Kamchatka, Bering reached the strait that is now named for him. However, he did not see the American coast. On his second expedition from Kamchatka in 1741, Bering captained a small wooden ship, the *Saint Peter*. On this journey, Bering did find the American coast, seeing Mount Saint Elias from the sea. On the return journey, Bering's ship was caught in terrible storms and wrecked on a deserted island. Bering and many other crew members died there of scurvy. The forty-six survivors built a rough new boat out of the *Saint Peter*'s timber and finally returned to Russia in 1742.

ALEKSANDR ANDREYEVICH BARANOV

FUR TRADER

BORN: *1747, Kargopol, Russia*
DIED: *April 16, 1819, Batavia, Java*

Aleksandr Baranov turned his fortunes around by moving to Alaska after his Russian business, located in Siberia, failed. In Alaska, Baranov established several profitable fur trading posts around Kodiak Island. In 1799, he was named the manager of the Russian American Company. This powerful position helped him govern all Russian activities in

North America. Baranov supported educational opportunities for Native Alaskans. He died while returning to Russia after spending twenty-eight years in Alaska.

JOE JUNEAU

PROSPECTOR

BORN: *unknown, 1826*
DIED: *1903, Dawson City, Canada*

In 1880, Joe Juneau and Richard Harris were just two prospectors in Alaska. They were lucky enough to follow the right lead. Following the advice of Chief Kowee, a member of the Auk Tlingit tribe, they discovered a huge lode of gold. "We knew it was gold," wrote one of the men in their party, "but so much, and not in particles; streaks running through the rock and little lumps as large as peas or beans." Juneau and Harris set up camp there in Silver Bow Basin. Their simple camp became the capital of the state. The town was first named Harrisburg and later renamed Rockwell. Determined to memorialize his own name, Juneau spent the bulk of his first earnings buying votes from his fellow miners. His heavy spending worked and they voted to rename the town Juneau.

JOHN MUIR

NATURALIST

BORN: *April 21, 1838, Dunbar, Scotland*
DIED: *December 24, 1914, Los Angeles, CA*

When John Muir was eleven, his family left Scotland and moved to Wisconsin. Even as a young man, he was enchanted by the forests and landscape of Wisconsin. As an adult, Muir shared his love of nature with a wide audience through his elegant writings and energetic explorations. His journeys took him through Canada, Cuba, Panama, Siberia, China, India, Europe, Egypt, Japan, New Zealand, and Australia. But Alaska's wilderness held a very special place for Muir. Muir's Glacier carries his name today, but his true legacy is the national park system and the Sierra Club, an institution he helped found. He wrote more than three hundred books and articles, including *Stickeen: The Story of a Dog* (1909) and *Travels in Alaska* (1915).

ROBERT WILLIAM SERVICE

POET

BORN: *January 16, 1874, Preston, England*
DIED: *September 11, 1958, Lancieux, France*

Two of the most famous poems about Alaska, "The Cremation of Sam McGee" and "The Shooting of Dan McGrew," were written by Robert William Service. Raised in Scotland, Service moved to Canada in 1894. His experiences in the Yukon provided inspiration for his first collection of poems, *Songs of a Sourdough* (1907). Service's popular poetry captured the rugged spirit of the people who loved life in Alaska. As a poet, he was determined to speak to common people. "The only society I like," he said, "is that which is rough and tough — and the tougher the better. That's where you get down to bedrock and meet human people." His collections of poetry include *Ballads of a Cheechako* (1909) and *Songs of the Far North* (1958).

Jack London

Writer

BORN: *January 12, 1876, San Francisco, CA*
DIED: *November 22, 1916, Santa Rosa, CA*

John Griffith (Jack) London's best-selling novels capture the grit and determination of people who face life head-on. London went to the Yukon in 1897 in search of gold. Instead, he found inspiration for his first collection of Klondike tales, *The Son of the Wolf* (1900). Two of London's most famous novels focus on animals in the far north. *The Call of the Wild* (1903) tells the tale of Buck, a dog who travels from California to the Yukon. *White Fang* (1906) describes a savage wolf who becomes domesticated. In addition to his novels, London also wrote passionate political articles.

Ernest Gruening

Politician

BORN: *February 6, 1886, New York, NY*
DIED: *January 26, 1974, Washington, D.C.*

Because of his dedication to helping Alaska become one of the United States, Ernest Gruening is known as "the father of Alaska statehood." Although trained as a doctor at Harvard Medical School, Gruening decided to become a journalist. He wrote articles and editorials for newspapers in Boston and New York. After serving with the Federal Artillery Corps during World War I, he returned to journalism. He became intrigued with another career: politics. Gruening spent several years with the U.S. delegation to Puerto Rico before joining the Alaska International Highway Commission in 1938. The next year, he was appointed governor of the Territory of Alaska, a post he held for fourteen years. In 1959, Gruening was the first U.S. Senator to represent the new state of Alaska. He served for ten years.

Elizabeth Peratrovich

Civil Rights Activist

BORN: *July 4, 1911, Petersburg*
DIED: *December 1, 1958, Juneau*

Elizabeth Peratrovich's commitment to fairness and justice contributed greatly to the passage of the first antidiscrimination law in the United States. Peratrovich experienced strong prejudice against her Tlingit heritage growing up in Alaska. In 1945, the Alaska senate was considering passing an antidiscrimination bill requiring equal treatment for all citizens applying for public housing. Using her position as Grand Camp President of the Alaska Native Sisterhood, Peratrovich gave a moving speech emphasizing the need for reform. The bill passed. Years later, the territory's governor, Ernest Gruening, said that without Peratrovich's vibrant speech, the measure would not have been accepted.

John Bell "Benny" Benson

Flag Designer

BORN: *1913, Chignik*
DIED: *July 2, 1972, Kodiak*

John Bell "Benny" Benson's heritage was part Swedish and part Aleut. At the age of thirteen, Benny Benson designed the Alaskan state flag. His design, which depicts the big dipper and north star in gold against a blue field, was selected from entries by more than seven hundred Alaskan schoolchildren. At the time of the contest, Benson was living in an orphanage in Seward. To explain his design, he wrote, "The blue in the flag is for the state flower (Forget-me-not) and the Alaskan sky. The gold is for the natural wealth. The Big Dipper and North Star are symbolic for Alaska's position in relation to the heavens." Benson won $1,000 and a gold watch engraved with the new flag.

Susan Butcher

Iditarod Champion

BORN: *December 26, 1956, Boston, MA*

Four-time winner of the Iditarod Trail Sled Dog Race, Susan Butcher has probably done more than any other person to popularize sled dog racing. Her phenomenal wins, in 1986, 1987, 1988, and 1990, won her fans around the world and amazed many people who thought that dog mushing was a sport for men only. Butcher owned her first sled dog as a child in Boston. Later, in Colorado, she managed a kennel of fifty sled dogs and four horses. Finally, in 1978, Butcher fulfilled her goal of racing in the Iditarod. Over the next years, she concentrated on sharpening her skills, training both herself and her team.

Tommy Moe

Alpine Skier

BORN: *February 17, 1970, Missoula, MT*

Downhill skier Tommy Moe was the first man from the United States to win two Olympic alpine skiing medals in one year. At the 1994 Winter Olympics in Lillehammer, Norway, Moe captured the gold medal in downhill and the silver medal in the Super Giant Slalom. He won the second medal on his twenty-fourth birthday.

As a teenager, Moe developed his impressive downhill skills at Glacier Creek Ski Academy in Girdwood, Alaska. Also an expert river guide, Moe is currently co-owner of Class V Whitewater, a rafting and kayaking vacation service. Moe still skies frequently and shares his knowledge by teaching. He spends his summers in Jackson Hole, Wyoming, but returns to Girdwood for the winter season.

Jewel

Singer and Poet

BORN: *May 23, 1974, Payson, UT*

Jewel Kilcher's unique voice has captured listeners' ears and hearts around the world. Jewel's family moved to Alaska when she was young. Jewel's mother encouraged her to explore her creativity, with music and lyrics. By the time she was six, Jewel was performing songs with her parents. However, it was a memorable performance of "Over the Rainbow" in 1989 on Tom Bodett's popular public radio program that launched her public career. Jewel's first album, *Pieces of You,* was released in 1995 and went platinum eleven times. Her follow-up CD, *Spirit*, sold even more copies.

Alaska

History At-A-Glance

Early 1700s
The Haida move from Canada into Tlingit territory in present-day Alaska.

1724
Russian czar Peter the Great commissions Vitus Bering to explore the route east of Siberia.

1728
Vitus Bering passes through the Bering Strait on his first voyage to America.

1741
On his second voyage, Vitus Bering lands on Kayak Island.

1802
Tlingits attack the Russian settlement in Sitka.

1804
Russians retaliate against the Tlingit and drive them from the region.

1821
Russia prohibits other countries from trading in Alaska.

1840
The Hudson's Bay Company establishes two trading posts in Alaska.

1853
Oil is discovered in Cook Inlet.

1867
The United States purchases Alaska from Russia for $7.2 million.

1879
The U.S. Navy assumes governmental control of Alaska.

1884
The Organic Act gives the territory a governor, laws, courts, and a school system.

1600 — 1700 — 180

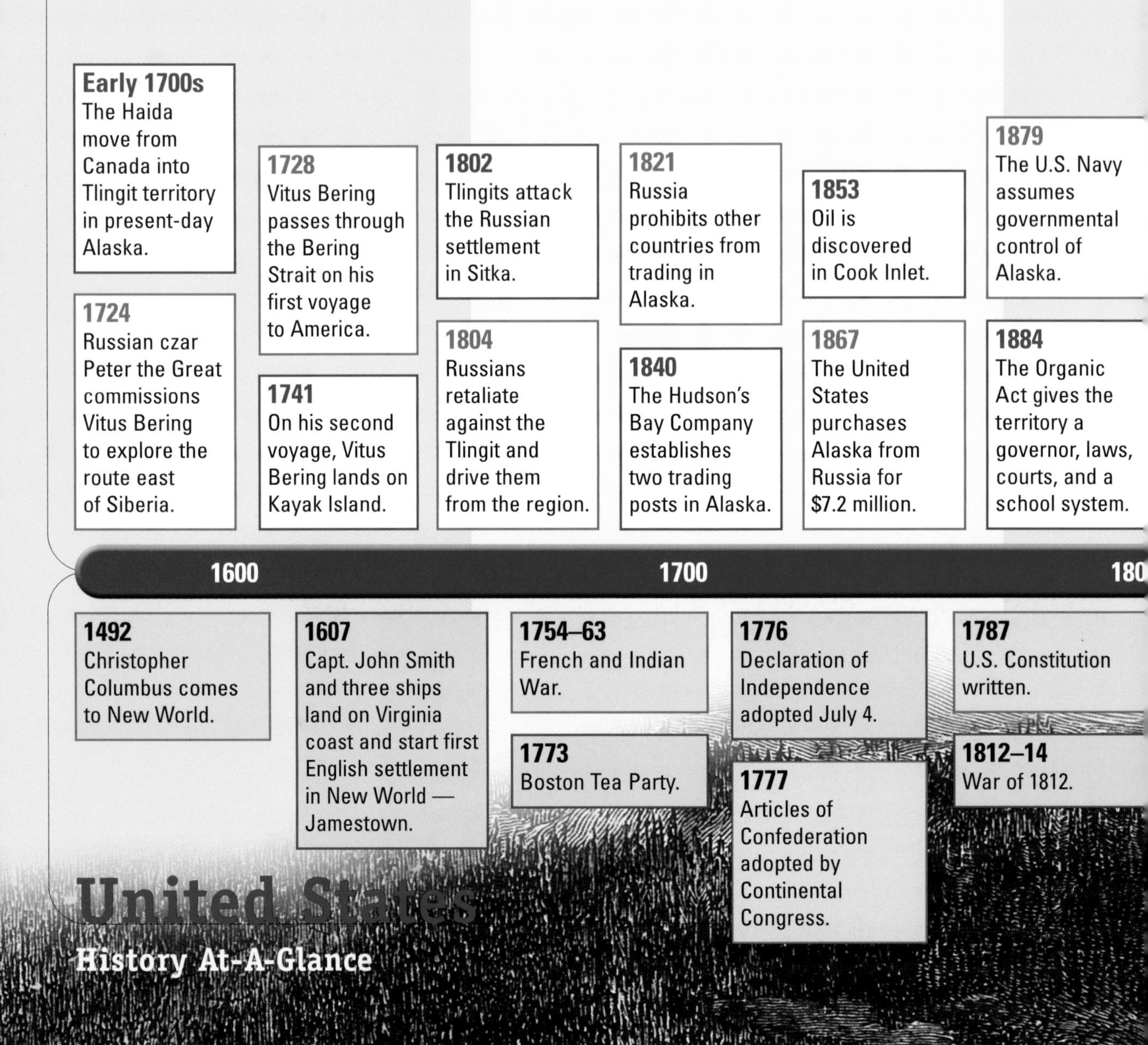

1492
Christopher Columbus comes to New World.

1607
Capt. John Smith and three ships land on Virginia coast and start first English settlement in New World — Jamestown.

1754–63
French and Indian War.

1773
Boston Tea Party.

1776
Declaration of Independence adopted July 4.

1777
Articles of Confederation adopted by Continental Congress.

1787
U.S. Constitution written.

1812–14
War of 1812.

United States

History At-A-Glance

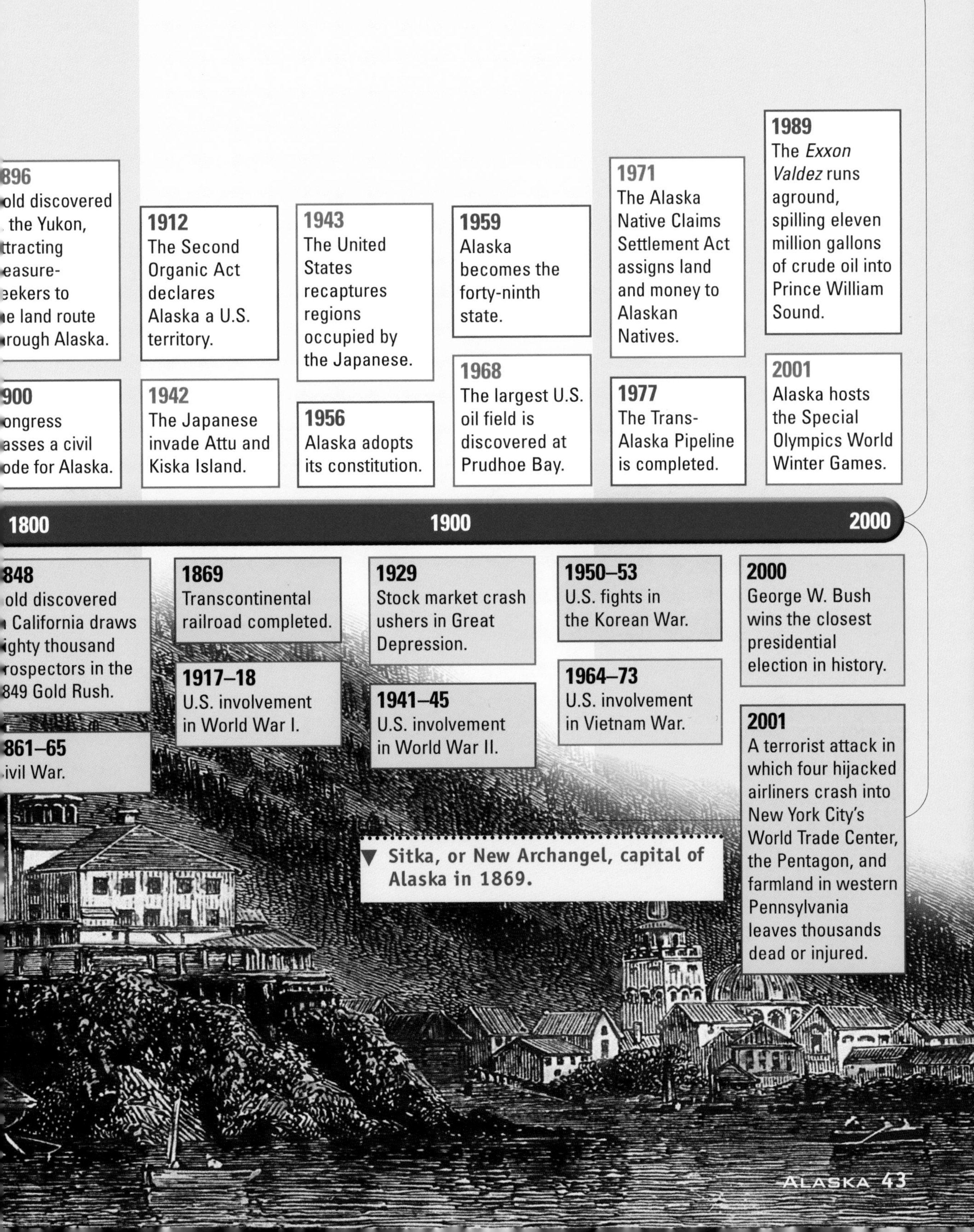

▼ Sitka, or New Archangel, capital of Alaska in 1869.

Festivals and Fun for All

Check web site for exact date and directions.

Alaska Bald Eagle Festival, Haines
Birdwatchers, photographers, and other nature lovers flock to Haines in Alaska's panhandle each November to watch as eagles (as many as three thousand) gather along a 4-mile (6.4 km) stretch of the Chilkat River.
www.baldeaglefest.org

Alaska Folk Festival, Juneau
Everyone from school groups to professional singers gets a chance to perform at this free annual musical celebration.
www.juneau.com/aff

Alaska State Fair, Palmer
Expect to be dazzled by Alaska's annual state fair featuring entertainment, games, rides, livestock, and exhibits. Displays and vendors highlight everything from giant vegetables to tasty Alaskan foods. Popular entertainers offer nightly shows.
www.alaskastatefair.org

Bear Paw Festival, Chugiak/Eagle River
This yearly festival includes an impressive parade as well as just-for-fun events, such as the Slippery Salmon Olympics and the Dog-Owner Look-Alike Contest.
www.cer.org/bear_paw_festival_profile.htm

Copper River Shorebird Festival, Cordova
This is one of Alaska's many birding festivals. It consistently attracts bird lovers and nature photographers to prime bird-viewing locations.
www.inalaska.com/features/ph/birdfestivals/birdingfestivals1.html

Fur Rendezvous, Anchorage
Since 1935, Anchorage has hosted this huge community fair. Now the largest winter festival in Alaska, the Fur Rendezvous includes the World Championship Sprint Sled Dog Race.
www.furrondy.net

Great Alaska Shootout, Anchorage
In November, Alaska hosts college basketball teams from throughout the country in an exciting tournament.
www.goseawolves.com

Harbor Stars Boat Parade, Kodiak
Majestic boats are the attraction at this unusual December parade, which pays tribute to the importance of water to Alaska's economy and culture.
www.alaska.com/akcom/southcentral/visit_travel/story/1141373p1256238c.html

Iditarod Trail Sled Dog Race, Anchorage to Nome

The most famous dog race in the world covers 1,150 miles (1,850 km) of traditional trails used by sled teams for many years. Crowds gather to cheer on the dogs and their mushers as they complete this grueling test of endurance.
www.iditarod.com

Kodiak Crab Festival, Kodiak

Each May, the crab festival highlights include a grand parade and an art show, featuring the works of local artists.
www.kodiak.org/crabfest.html

Mayor's Midnight Sun Marathon, Anchorage

Cheer on forty-five hundred runners as they race 26.2 miles (42.2 km) through downtown Anchorage and into the Chugach Foothills.
www.mayorsmarathon.com

Midnight Sun Festival and Softball Tournament, Nome

Twenty-two hours of direct sunlight (and two hours of twilight) give visitors to Nome plenty of time to enjoy themselves. Where else is softball played at midnight without artificial lights?
www.alaska.com/akcom/southcentral/visit_travel/story/1141373p-1256231c.html

Nalukataq, Barrow

This traditional festival is held by Inupiat Eskimos to celebrate the end of a successful whaling season. This joyful Native holiday can last for days, often including games, ceremonies, and feasts.
www.co.north-slope.ak.us/ihlchome/_private/pages/overview/overview.htm

Polar Bear Swim, Nome

On Memorial Day, brave swimmers plunge into the icy waters of the Bering Sea.
www.alaska.com/akcom/western/visit_travel/story/632797p-697276c.html

Savoonga Walrus Festival, St. Lawrence Island

Each May, Alaskan Eskimos celebrate a traditional springtime festival.
www.awrta.org/communities.cfm?city=Savoonga

World Eskimo-Indian Olympics, Fairbanks

Native Alaskans compete in traditional events that display strength, speed, and endurance.
www.weio.org/History.html

World Extreme Skiing Championship, Valdez

Daredevil skiers from around the world come to Valdez every spring to compete in these thrilling races and competitions.
www.whatsgoingon.com/100things.cgi/extreme/

World Ice Art Championships, Fairbanks

Watch talented competitors carve astonishing ice sculptures out of ice. The impressive creations are left on display as they slowly melt in the Sun.
www.icealaska.com

▶ Visitors enjoy a salmon bake at one of Alaska's many festivals.

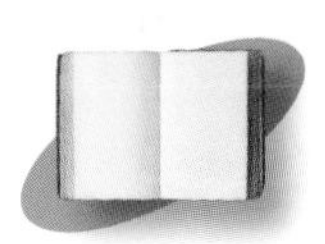

Books

Bodett, Tom. *Williwaw!* New York: Knopf, 1999. Meet Ivan and September Crane, a brother and sister waiting on a remote Alaskan Island for their father to return from his fishing. Their exciting adventures thrill readers while they also learn about life in Alaska.

Dils, Tracey. *The Exxon Valdez (Great Disasters: Reforms and Ramifications).* New York: Chelsea House, 2001. Read a detailed account of the huge oil spill at Prudhoe Bay. Learn about the aftermath of the disaster, including attempts to clean the water and ensure the region's safety from future disasters.

Fremon, David K. *The Alaska Purchase in American History.* Berkeley Heights, NJ: Enslow, 1999. This fascinating historical account describes the people who made "Seward's Folly" a part of the United States.

Hobbs, Will. *Jason's Gold.* New York: Morrow Junior, 1999. This exciting historical novel views the events of the 1897 Gold Rush from the viewpoint of fifteen-year-old Jason Hawthorn.

Oman, Lela Kiana. *The Epic of Qayaq: The Longest Story Ever Told by My People.* Ottawa, Canada: Carleton University Press, 1996. Oman retells the traditional origins tale of the Inupiaq people of the Kobuk Valley. Inuit art illustrates this tale of a hero's adventures in Alaska.

Wilson, Ian, and Sally Wilson. *Gold Rush: North to Alaska and the Klondike.* Vancouver, Canada: Gordon Soules, 1997. Follow along as the authors re-create the trails and hardships experienced by the bold travelers who hiked Chikoot Pass to search for gold in the Yukon.

Web Sites

▶ Official state web site
www.state.ak.us

▶ About Alaska
www.alaska.com

▶ Alaska Almanac
www.netstate.com/states/alma/ak_alma.htm

▶ National Parks in Alaska
www.nps.gov/akso/

▶ Alaska Historical Society
www.alaskahistoricalsociety.org

Note: Page numbers in *italics* refer to maps, illustrations, or photographs.